FOSSIL FUELS

DiscoverRoo
An Imprint of Pop!
popbooksonline.com

Christopher Forest

abdobooks.com

Published by Pop!, a division of ABDO, PO Box 398166, Minneapolis, Minnesota 55439. Copyright © 2020 by POP, LLC. International copyrights reserved in all countries. No part of this book may be reproduced in any form without written permission from the publisher. Pop!™ is a trademark and logo of POP, LLC.

Printed in the United States of America, North Mankato, Minnesota.

102019
012020

THIS BOOK CONTAINS RECYCLED MATERIALS

Cover Photo: iStockphoto
Interior Photos: iStockphoto, 1, 5, 6, 12, 13, 17, 18, 21, 22 (top), 23 (bottom), 31; Shutterstock Images, 7, 9, 11, 14, 15, 19, 20, 26, 27, 28–29, 30; The Keasbury-Gordon Photograph Archive/KGPA Ltd/Alamy, 22 (bottom); JT Vintage/Glasshouse Images/Alamy, 23 (top); Johnny Greig/Alamy, 25

Editor: Sophie Geister-Jones
Series Designer: Jake Slavik

Library of Congress Control Number: 2019942602
Publisher's Cataloging-in-Publication Data

Names: Forest, Christopher, author.

Title: Fossil fuels / by Christopher Forest

Description: Minneapolis, Minnesota : Pop!, 2020 | Series: Natural resources | Includes online resources and index.

Identifiers: ISBN 9781532165849 (lib. bdg.) | ISBN 9781532167164 (ebook)

Subjects: LCSH: Fossil fuels--Juvenile literature. | Natural resources--Juvenile literature. | Environment--Juvenile literature. | Ecology--Juvenile literature. | Petroleum supply--Juvenile literature.

Classification: DDC 333.82--dc23

WELCOME TO DiscoverRoo!

Pop open this book and you'll find QR codes loaded

with information, so you can learn even more!

Scan this code* and others

like it while you read, or visit

the website below to make

this book pop!

popbooksonline.com/fossil-fuels

*Scanning QR codes requires a web-enabled smart device with a QR code reader app and a camera.

TABLE OF CONTENTS

CHAPTER 1
A LOOK AT FOSSIL FUELS

A woman drives her car home after work. She turns on the lights in her kitchen. Then she uses the stove to cook dinner. All these tasks use fossil fuels.

WATCH A VIDEO HERE!

Most cars use gasoline, which is made from fossil fuels.

Fossil fuels include coal, oil, and natural gas. These fuels are important sources of energy. They provide heat for homes and fuel for vehicles. People also use them to create electricity.

Many airplane engines use kerosene, a fuel made from oil.

DID YOU KNOW?

More than three-fourths of the energy in the world comes from fossil fuels.

Fossil fuels come from the ancient remains of animals and plants. These plants and animals died long ago. Ocean water covered some of them. Others were buried in soil. Over time, layers of rock formed above them. The remains became buried deep underground. As heat and pressure built up, the remains slowly turned into fuel.

FOSSIL FUEL FORMATION

1 Ocean plants and animals die.

2 Their remains are pressed underground.

3 Oil and natural gas form.

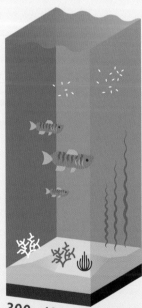

300–400 million years ago

100 million years ago

today

CHAPTER 2
TYPES AND USES

People use fossil fuels in many ways.

For example, natural gas is often used

to create heat or electricity. This fuel

is found deep underground. People drill

into rocks to bring it up to the surface.

LEARN MORE
HERE!

Natural gas can be found all over the world, beneath land and water.

A coal mine's tunnels can stretch many miles below ground.

Coal formed from plants and animals that lived in ancient swamps. People dig mines to reach it. Many power plants burn coal. They use energy created from burning coal to produce electricity.

DID YOU KNOW? The United States and Russia have the largest coal deposits in the world.

Oil formed from plants and animals in ancient oceans. Their remains settled to the seafloor. Over time, some parts of

At a refinery, machines turn oil into other fuels, such as petroleum or kerosene.

these oceans dried up. As a result, lots

of oil can be found below land and at sea.

Humans drill wells to get oil. Then

they **refine** it to produce petroleum.

People use petroleum as fuel for cars. It

is also used to

make plastic.

Balloons are one of approximately 6,000 everyday items made from fossil fuels.

CHAPTER 3

CURRENT CHALLENGES

Fossil fuels are very useful. But they can cause problems. The first challenge is supply. Fossil fuels are not renewable. Earth has limited amounts. And people can only get them in certain places.

COMPLETE AN ACTIVITY HERE!

Offshore oil rigs can drill more than 3,500 feet (1,000 m) below the surface.

Pipelines are a common way to send fuels to the people who use them.

Some countries have more fossil fuels than others. As a result, fuel can be hard for some people to get. Someday, the supply will run out completely.

Pipelines sometimes leak, spilling oil into the water and land around them.

Coal plants release harmful pollutants, such as mercury and lead, into the air.

Fossil fuels can also damage the **environment**. When people burn fossil fuels, smoke and chemicals enter the air. This **pollution** is bad for the planet. It harms people, plants, and

CLIMATE CHANGE

Earth's **atmosphere** contains gases that trap heat. It keeps the planet warm enough to support life. But in recent years, Earth's average temperature has been rising. Weather has been affected too. Using fossil fuels caused these changes. Fossil fuels release carbon dioxide when they burn. This gas traps heat. Adding more carbon dioxide to the air traps more heat.

animals. Pollution also contributes to climate change. For instance, it adds **carbon dioxide** to the air.

USING FOSSIL FUELS

1821
The world's first natural gas well is drilled in Fredonia, New York.

200 BCE
People first begin mining coal.

1690 CE
Coal replaces wood as the main fuel used in Europe.

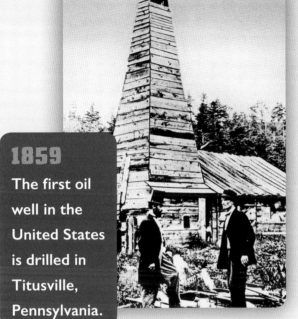

1859
The first oil well in the United States is drilled in Titusville, Pennsylvania.

2017
Approximately 62 percent of the electricity used in the United States comes from burning fossil fuels.

1956
Oil replaces coal as the main fuel used in the United States.

CHAPTER 4
FUEL FOR THE FUTURE

No one is sure how long the supply of fossil fuels will last. But they do know these fuels cannot be easily replaced. The fuels take millions of years to form. People must work to **conserve** them.

LEARN MORE HERE!

WAST OIL

The United States is the largest consumer of oil in the world.

Many countries make laws and goals

to limit fuel use. Families can also help.

They can unplug electronics when not

using them. And they can keep their heat

Charging electronic devices uses fossil
fuels. So does creating the materials these
devices are made of.

Turning off lights when they are not being used helps conserve energy.

low when they are not home. These

actions conserve electricity. Using less

energy means using less fuel.

Scientists are finding other sources

of energy. Many are renewable. These

sources include water, wind, and sunlight.

Unlike fossil fuels, they will not run out.

They also tend to be better for the

Solar panels and wind turbines are two sources of renewable energy.

planet. Most renewable sources do not

create **carbon dioxide**. They also

cause less **pollution**.

DID YOU KNOW? The United States doubled its use of renewable energy between 2000 and 2018.

MAKING CONNECTIONS

TEXT-TO-SELF

Fossil fuels are used to produce electricity. How would your life be different without electricity?

TEXT-TO-TEXT

Have you read other books about energy? What problems and benefits did those books describe?

TEXT-TO-WORLD

People around the world are working to conserve fossil fuels. What is one way your family or community could use less energy?

GLOSSARY

atmosphere – the layers of gases that surround a planet.

carbon dioxide – a gas that is produced when fossil fuels burn.

conserve – to save and not waste.

environment – the natural surroundings where plants and animals live.

pollution – harmful substances that collect in the air, water, or soil.

refine – to make something purer by removing chemicals or waste.

INDEX

ONLINE RESOURCES
popbooksonline.com

Scan this code* and others like it while you read, or visit the website below to make this book pop!

popbooksonline.com/fossil-fuels

*Scanning QR codes requires a web-enabled smart device with a QR code reader app and a camera.